MADAM I'M ADAM

LLEWD DID I LIVE HANNH,
EVIL I DID DWELL.

MADAM I'M ADAM

···· AND ····

OTHER PALINDROMES

WRITTEN BY

WILLIAM IRVINE

ILLUSTRATED BY

STEVEN GUARNACCIA

CHARLES SCRIBNER'S SONS   NEW YORK

Charles Scribner's Sons
Macmillan Publishing Company
866 Third Avenue, New York, NY 10022
Collier Macmillan Canada, Inc.

Library of Congress Cataloging-in-Publication Data
Irvine, William, 1958–
Madam I'm Adam and other palindromes.
I. Palindromes. I. Guarnaccia, Steven. II. Title.
PN6371.I78 1987   793.7'3   87–16652
ISBN 0–684–18850–3

Macmillan books are available at special discounts for bulk purchases
for sales promotions, premiums, fund-raising, or educational use.
For details, contact:
Special Sales Director
Macmillan Publishing Company
866 Third Avenue
New York, NY 10022

10 9 8 7 6 5 4 3 2 1

Printed in the United States of America

Introduction

It all started many years ago, when I discovered a mysterious connection between TUMS and SMUT. I remember gazing at the small roll of antacid tablets with a new sense of awe and wonderment. "This could be no coincidence, no random occurrence," I thought to myself. "It is a talisman. There must be others." Back in the 1960s, when a young lad's mind was encouraged to wander in all sorts of strange directions, mine was hell-bent on the backwards. I soon started to read everything the wrong way intentionally. I would practice religiously on street signs (POTS) and bill-boards (A TOYOTA) and by the time I had finished school, I could read a mean streak in both directions. This totally useless talent has led to a lifelong interest in collecting and inventing palindromes, phrases that read the same backwards as they do forwards. Everyone knows a few of them—MADAM I'M ADAM, or RADAR—but there are many more lesser-known and newly minted examples that deserve the attention of the wordly wise, and that is how this book came about.

There are several things to keep in mind when you are creating a palindrome. First, it is not as easy as it looks and you must be extremely patient. There are but a tiny number of word combinations that work palindromically, and of these only a small number make any sense at all without a frame of reference. So, unless you know that you are reading a memo from a New Guinean decorator, R. E.: PAPUA ETAGERE GATEAU PAPER doesn't mean very much. Nor, for that matter, does SATAN, OSCILLATE MY METALLIC SONATAS (an electronic music composer in Hell?), or that exotic African entree, EMU FAT SAP PASTA FUME. Or AMARYLLIS SILLYRAMA (a discotheque for hothouse flowers?). This particular genre would not exist without the unfailing efforts of Leigh Mercer and J. A. Lindon, British palindromists who have invented hundreds of nonsensical gems. We are indebted to Mr. Lindon for such inspired creations as DEIRDRE WETS ALTAR OF ST. SIMON'S—NO MISTS, FOR AT LAST EWER DRIED, and the ever-popular JAR A TONGA, NAG NOT A RAJ.

This is not as easy as it looks. There are few palindromes of any length that can stand alone. The late John Ciardi received the following submission from a reader of his popular column in the old *Saturday Review:*

COPYWRITERS SHOULD LEARN TO CONVEY THEIR IDEAS CLEARLY AND INCISIVELY WITHOUT USING GOBBLEDYGOOK THAT SOUNDS LIKE EKIL SDNUOS TAHT KOOGYDELBBOG GNISU TUOHTIW YLEVISICNI DNA YLRAELC SAEDI RIEHT YEVNOC OT NRAEL DLUOHS SRETIRWYPOC.

You could, of course, write hundreds of these yourself, but I would challenge you to create something similar to my favorite palindrome, composed by the writer Alastair Reid:

T. ELIOT, TOP BARD, NOTES PUTRID TANG EMANATING, IS SAD. "I'D ASSIGN IT A NAME: GNAT DIRT UPSET ON DRAB POT TOILET."

Because most articles and prepositions are, by construction, excluded from the palindromic universe, there are an unusually large number of examples that sound like sensational newspaper headlines or strange commands: Hence, RAT IS SITAR and PART-SEMITE TIMES TRAP. This is a virtually unavoidable pitfall, and marks the style of many palindromes. Generally, the most successful compositions are remarkable for their brevity and simplicity: STRAW WARTS, for example, or GOLD-ENROD-ADORNED LOG. The fledgling palindromist should avoid the temptation of trying to improve his creation by increasing its length.

The attribution of palindromes is a perennial puzzle. Although there have been writers of them since Sotades completed his first palindromic sonnet in the third century B.C., most subsequent authors have been anonymous. Palindromists are in general so modest that they often deny authorship, and this has resulted in the misattribution of many examples that have been handed down to us. The well-known ABLE WAS I, ERE I SAW ELBA, for example, is conveniently attributed to Napoleon, whose knowledge of English wordplay was certainly questionable, at best.

But English is not the only source of backward exotica. Latin is particularly fertile ground for palindromes, yielding SUBI DURA A RUDIBUS (endure rough treatment from uncultured brutes) and SATOR AREPO TENET OPERA ROTAS (the sower Arepo works with the help of a wheel). And Welsh gives us LLADD DAFAD DDALL (kill a blind sheep). We must not overlook SAIPPUAKAUPPIAS, the Finnish word for soap dealer. In any language, the palindrome is an exotic flower in the garden of wordplay. At least half the fun of the palindrome is its random celebration of the absurd, and it is in this spirit that this book is presented.

—WILLIAM IRVINE

STELLA WON NO WALLETS

VIVA LE TÉ DE TEL AVIV

STAB NAIL AT ILL ITALIAN BATS

RENO LONER

WE SEVEN, EVE, SEW

U.F.O. TOFU

EGAD! NO BONDAGE!

TUNA NUT

REFLOG A GOLFER

SIT ON A POTATO PAN, OTIS

LAGER, SIR, IS REGAL

PAGANINI: DIN IN A GAP

SENILE FELINES

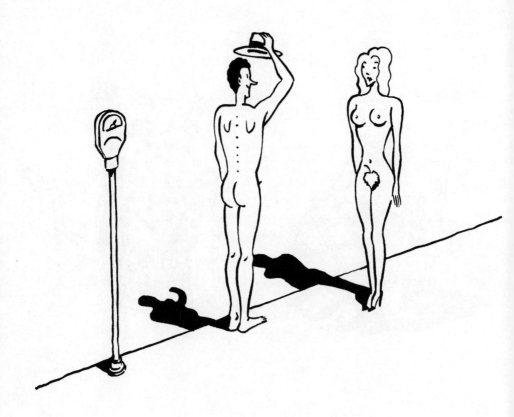

MADAM, I'M ADAM

TRAFALGAR RAG: *LA FART*

SORE EYE, EROS?

Egad, an adage!

KAYAK SALAD—ALASKA YAK

MUST SELL AT TALLEST SUM

MA IS A NUN, AS I AM

So, Ida, adios!

No lemons, no melon

LAY A WALLABY BABY BALL AWAY, AL

SEX AT NOON TAXES

SEX-AWARE ERA WAXES

NOW NED, I AM A MAIDEN NUN: NED, I AM A MAIDEN WON

NOG ERODED OREGON

EROS? SIDNEY, MY END IS SORE

YELL UPSET A CIDER: PREDICATES PULLEY

"M" LAB MENIAL SLAIN: EMBALM

GOD! A RED NUGGET! A FAT EGG UNDER A DOG!

BIRD RIB

TARZAN RAISED DESI ARNAZ' RAT

ENID AND EDNA DINE

LEPERS REPEL

RED NEVADA VENDER

SNIFF'UM MUFFINS

STOP! MURDER US NOT, TONSURED RUMPOTS

MAY A MOODY BABY DOOM A YAM?

SOLO GIGOLOS

NED, GO GAG OGDEN

STRATAGEM: MEGATARTS

GUSTAV KLIMT MILK VATS—UG!

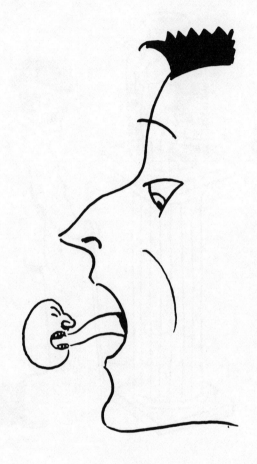

EVIL OLIVE

SIS, SARGASSO MOSS A GRASS IS

GNU DUNG

AH, SATAN SEES NATASHA

Rococo "R"

AL LETS DELLA CALL ED STELLA

A DOG! A PANIC IN A PAGODA!

CAMUS SEES SUMAC

STAR COMEDY BY DEMOCRATS

DENIM AXES EXAMINED

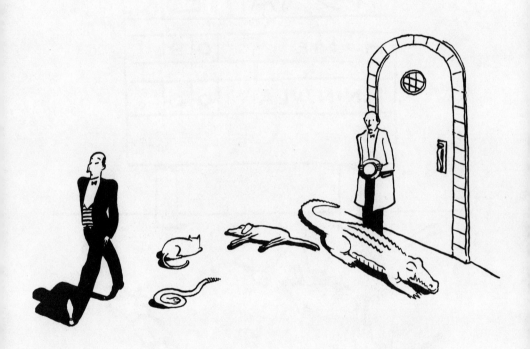

STEP ON NO PETS

DAEDALUS: NINE, PENINSULA: DEAD

A SLUT NIXES SEX IN TULSA

NEVER ODD OR EVEN

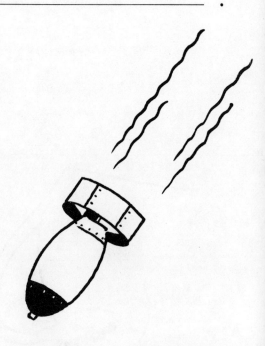

BOMBARD A DRAB MOB

DAIRY MYRIAD

DIOR DROID

DRAW, O COWARD!

MAYHEM, EH YAM?

LAMINATED E. T. ANIMAL

I MAIM MIAMI

SH, TOM SEES MOTHS!

PARTY BOOBYTRAP

A MAN, A PLAN, A CANAL—PANAMA

O.E.D. OR RODEO?

NOSEGAY AGES ON

dmc

WILLIAM IRVINE is a former editor and contributor to _Avenue Magazine_. His work has also appeared in _The American Spectator_. This is his first book.

STEVEN GUARNACCIA is an illustrator whose drawings have appeared on book jackets, masks for Apple computers, T-shirts for SWATCH, and in publications here and abroad. He is also the illustrator of _Jonathan's Cloud_, a children's book, and the forthcoming _Jeremy Sage's Birthday Book_.